SPACE
UNIVERSITY™

THE SPACE
EXPLORER'S
GUIDE TO

Planets, Moons, and More!

BY

MEGAN GENDELL AND KAREN DE SEVE

WITH **RACHEL CONNOLLY**
SPACE EDUCATOR

RYAN WYATT
VISUAL ADVISOR

AND **JIM SWEITZER**, PH.D.
NASA SCIENCE CENTER,
DEPAUL UNIVERSITY

SCHOLASTIC INC.

NEW YORK   TORONTO   LONDON   AUCKLAND   SYDNEY
MEXICO CITY   NEW DELHI   HONG KONG   BUENOS AIRES

Who's Who at Space U

Megan Gendell
Writer
Megan is an assistant editor who helps keep things running smoothly at Space U Mission Control.

Karen de Seve
Writer
Karen writes text for exhibits at the American Museum of Natural History in New York City. She has also written for Scholastic magazines.

Ryan Wyatt
Visual Advisor
Ryan designs scientific visuals for the American Museum of Natural History's Rose Center for Earth and Space.

Rachel Connolly
Consultant
Rachel manages the astrophysics education program at the American Museum of Natural History's Rose Center for Earth and Space.

Jim Sweitzer
Advisor
Jim is an astrophysicist and the director of the NASA Space Science Center at DePaul University in Chicago.

ISBN: 0-439-55743-7

Copyright © 2004 by Scholastic Inc.

Editor: Andrea Menotti
Designers: Peggy Gardner, Lee Kaplan, Tricia Kleinot
Illustrators: Daniel Aycock, Yancey C. Labat, Thomas Nakid, Ed Shems

Photos:
Front cover: A true-color picture of Saturn (image by NASA/JPL)
Back cover: A close-up view of Jupiter's Great Red Spot (image by NASA/JPL)
Title page: A view of Mars, showing the entire Valles Marineris canyon (image by NASA/USGS)

All photos are NASA/JPL images unless otherwise noted.
Pages 5, 11, and 15: (Mars) NASA/STScI/Colorado/Cornell/SSI. Pages 5, 10, 15, and 30: (Jupiter) NASA/JPL/USGS.
Pages 5 and 41: (Io) PIRL/University of Arizona. Page 7: Mike Garlick/Photo Researchers. Page 8: NASA/C. R. O'Dell/
Vanderbilt. Pages 9, 11, 14, and 22: (Earth) NASA/R. Stöckli/Robert Simmon/GSFC/MODIS. Page 11: (Sun) NSO/AURA/NSF,
(Copernicus) Photo Researchers. Pages 11 and 14: (Mercury) NASA/JPL/Northwestern University. Pages 14 and 33: (Saturn)
NASA/STScI/AURA. Page 16: (crater) NASA/JPL/Northwestern University, (Mariner) NASA. Page 19: (Magellan) NASA.
Page 24: (Mars) NASA/JPL/USGS. Pages 28 and 29: (asteroids) Johns Hopkins University/Applied Physics Laboratory.
Pages 29 and 48 (Spot the Dot): Michael Richmond. Page 31, Cosmic Viewer 1 and 3 (Jupiter): NASA/JPL/University
of Arizona; Cosmic Viewer 2: (Jupiter) NASA/STScI/AURA, (Europa) NASA/DLR. Page 37: (Cosmic Viewer) NASA/JPL/USGS.
Page 39: (Dr. Tyson) Harry Heliotis, (AMNH) Denis Finnin. Page 40: (our Moon and Triton) NASA/JPL/USGS.
Page 41: (Europa) NASA/DLR. Page 42: (top) Harvard College Observatory/Photo Researchers,
(Cosmic Viewer) Axel Mellinger. Page 44: (Dr. Oppenheimer) AMNH.

12 11 10 9 8 7 6 5 4 3 2 1   3 4 5 6 7 8/0

Printed in the U.S.A.

First Scholastic printing, February 2004

The publisher has made every effort to ensure that the activities in this book are safe when done as instructed.
Adults should provide guidance and supervision whenever the activity requires.

Table of **Contents**

Solar System

Hey, cadet—ready for another Space U adventure? This month you'll get to check out plenty of planets, many moons, and lots of other wonders that whirl around our solar system! You'll be exploring questions like:

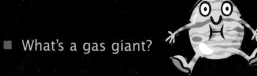

■ How did our solar system form?

■ What's a gas giant?

■ Why are planets different colors?

■ Which planet is rusty?

■ Which planet was once called George?

■ Which planet spins on its side?

■ What makes Venus such a hot place?

■ What's an asteroid belt?

■ Is Pluto really a planet?

■ How do we find planets beyond our solar system?

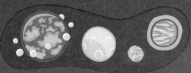

WHAT IS A PLANET, ANYWAY?

To answer this question, let's start with a quick quiz.

The word "planet" comes from an ancient Greek word that means:
  a) Big beautiful blob   **b)** Relatively round rock   **c)** Wanderer

Sensations!

Did you answer C? Then you got it! The word "planet" actually has nothing to do with what planets are made of—it has to do with how ancient people saw the planets moving, or *wandering*, across the sky.

Planets look like points of light in the night sky, like stars (but unlike stars, which shine with their own light, planets shine because they're reflecting light from the Sun, just like the Moon does).

Ancient Greeks noticed that these points of light seemed to move differently, or *wander*, in relation to the stars. At first people thought that these *wanderers* were orbiting around the Earth. It took thousands of years of watching the sky closely before astronomers figured out that these planets were orbiting the *Sun*, not the Earth. Suddenly our planet wasn't so special—it was just one of many planets that went around the Sun.

Planets come in all sorts of sizes and varieties— and that means it's sometimes hard to decide whether an object that's orbiting our Sun is a *planet* or just another hunk of rock in space! You'll see how tough it can be when you join in the raging debate over Pluto on page 38!

AND WHAT'S A MOON?

A moon is a *satellite* of a planet—that is, an object that orbits around a planet (a moon is a *natural* satellite, not one of those metal man-made ones!). We've got just *one* moon traveling around Earth, but planets can have ten moons...or sixty... or maybe more! Just like planets, moons come in many different sizes and can have lots of different features—like craters, volcanoes, and even ice-covered oceans!

AND WHAT ELSE HANGS AROUND OUR SOLAR SYSTEM?

Oh, there are big hunks of space rock called asteroids, huge dirty snowballs called comets, and who knows what else you might find? Just turn the page to launch your solar system adventure!

Your solar system tour would not be complete without great sightseeing opportunities, and that's what your new 3-D Cosmic Viewer is for! Slip in the discs, and you'll be transported to the surface of Mars, to the moons of Jupiter, and beyond— in three amazing dimensions! The Space U Interplanetary Express is boarding on page 14— pack your viewer and prepare for launch!

How to Get the *Best* View

When using your Cosmic Viewer, make sure to look at each image for a couple of seconds to give your eyes a chance to get used to the 3-D. It takes a little while to see all three dimensions in full effect!

THE SPACE UNIVERSITY WEB SITE

Visit www.scholastic.com/space for more fun with planets, moons, and more! You can design your own planets and discover some asteroids! Just don't forget this month's password—you'll need it to access the new episode!

PLANET PASSWORD

This month's web site password is:

PLANETFUN

Complete the missions in the *Planets, Moons, and More* episode to earn your personalized mission patch! Then print it out, cut it out, and paste it here!

Let's go waaaaaay back in time—billions of years back—to the time before our solar system was born.

Imagine the scene: A huge cloud of dust and gas is quietly hanging out in our galaxy, when…Bam! Suddenly a nearby supernova (an exploding star) gives the cloud a kick, and it begins to collapse and swirl.

The swirling cloud is called a *solar nebula*, and inside it are all the ingredients necessary to make everything in our solar system—including the planets, moons, asteroids, comets, you, your family, your friends, and all your favorite things! But right now all that stuff is just specks of dust and wisps of gas, whirling around, crashing and smashing together! Turn the page to find out what happens next!

So, what's going on inside the spinning solar nebula? Let's step into the kitchen with Chef Dustin Gass and see what's cookin'!

Cook up your very own solar system!

Grab your apron and let's get started!

CHEF DUSTIN GASS

Ingredients:

- Gravity
- Hydrogen gas
- Bits of rock and ice
- Dashes of oxygen, nitrogen, carbon, silicon, iron, and other elements

Step 1:

Turn on the Sun to heat your nebula.

Step 2:

Mix up the ingredients. Spin the mixture using gravity until a nice disk forms.

Step 3:

As the mixture spins, the ingredients will clump together. Allow the clumps to grow larger and larger until each clump is a baby planet. (Be patient: This will take about half a billion years!)

Step 4:

As the clumps grow into baby planets, their gravity will pull in any nearby bits of rock. Soon, you'll get nice big round planets going around the Sun with just a few million crumbs leftover (in the form of asteroids and comets). Your solar system is ready!

So, there you have it! That's what happens inside the solar nebula. To find out more about how the baby planets grow up, read on!

It's a
Bouncing Baby Planet!

As you've seen, the whirling solar nebula is not a very peaceful place for baby planets. There's lots of rock flying and crashing around—but who said growing up was easy!

Now here's the burning question that inquiring cadets will be asking: How did we get nice round planets of all different sizes and varieties from all that crazy swirling and smashing? Here's how!

IF YOU CAN'T TAKE THE HEAT...

The planets of our solar system all grew up differently because of the way the ingredients of the solar nebula were spread out.

You know the expression "If you can't take the heat, then get out of the kitchen"? Well, that's what happened to the light gases in the solar nebula. They couldn't take the heat near the Sun, so they got blown farther out, where they clustered around the newly forming planets Jupiter, Saturn, Uranus, and Neptune. These outer planets are called "gas giants" because of all the gases swirling around them. The inner planets—Mercury, Venus, Earth, and Mars—are made mostly of rock and metal.

LAYER IT ON!

How do baby planets get crusts and cores and all the layers in between? One word: HEAT! When you rub your hands together, you can feel them heating up—this heat is caused by *friction*. In the same way, when rocks crash into a baby planet, the baby planet grows hotter and hotter.

All that heat causes the baby planet to get melted and gooey inside, which means that the different ingredients can move around inside the planet. The heavy rock and metals mostly sink to the center, and the lighter materials float to the top and cool into a crusty surface. That's how a planet gets its layers!

Shape Up!

And how do the planets take shape? One word: GRAVITY! As the planets grow more massive, they gain more gravity, and that means they get stronger. Their gravity pulls in all directions, gathering the planets into ball shapes.

If you want to see this process in action, just scoop yourself a bowl of chocolate chip ice cream and watch it melt. See how the heavy chips sink to the bottom? That's the idea!

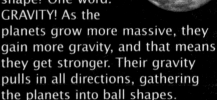

The SOLAR SYSTEM

Phew! After all that whirling and crashing, here's a diagram of how our solar system looks today!

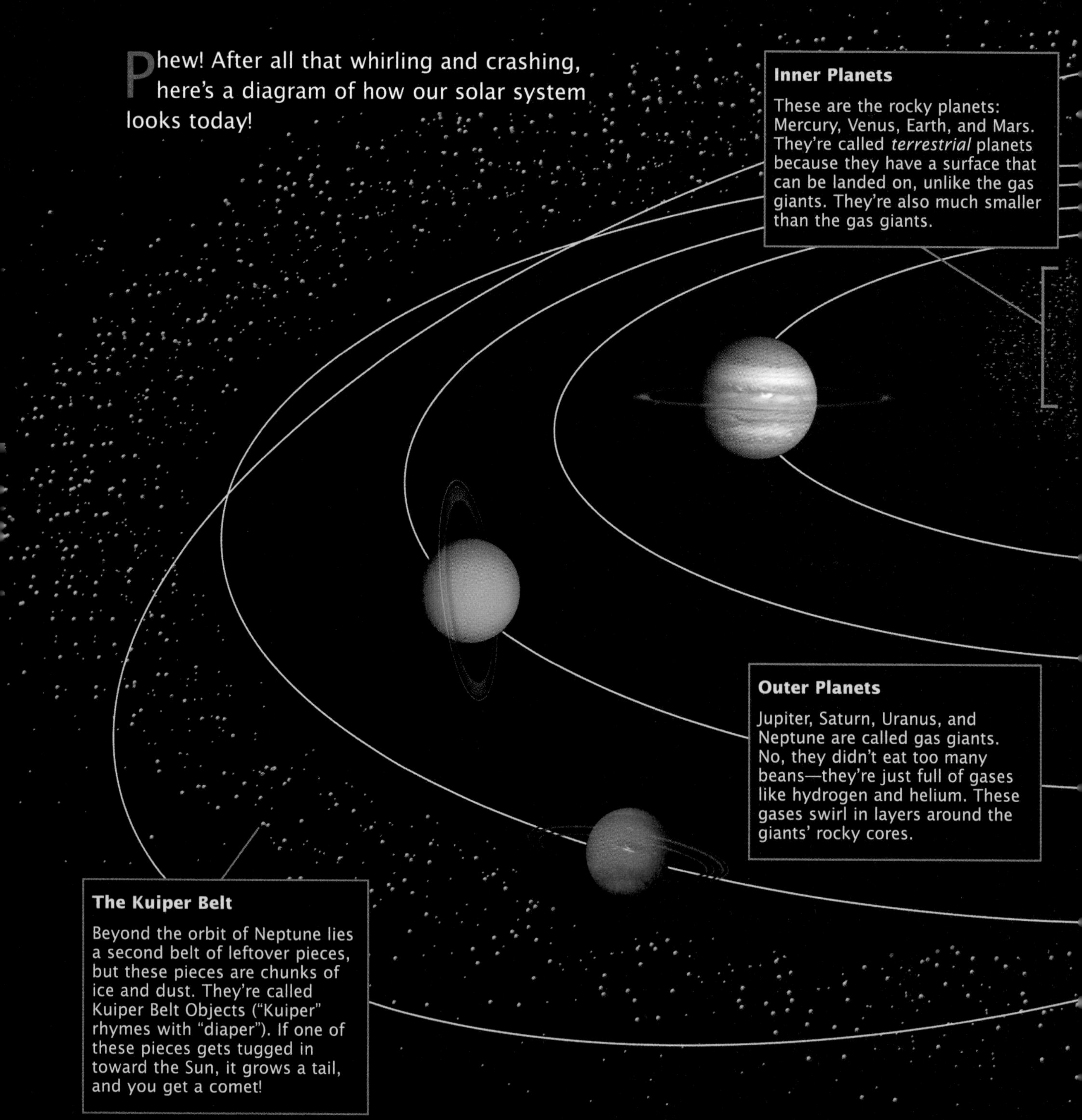

Inner Planets

These are the rocky planets: Mercury, Venus, Earth, and Mars. They're called *terrestrial* planets because they have a surface that can be landed on, unlike the gas giants. They're also much smaller than the gas giants.

Outer Planets

Jupiter, Saturn, Uranus, and Neptune are called gas giants. No, they didn't eat too many beans—they're just full of gases like hydrogen and helium. These gases swirl in layers around the giants' rocky cores.

The Kuiper Belt

Beyond the orbit of Neptune lies a second belt of leftover pieces, but these pieces are chunks of ice and dust. They're called Kuiper Belt Objects ("Kuiper" rhymes with "diaper"). If one of these pieces gets tugged in toward the Sun, it grows a tail, and you get a comet!

The Sun

The Sun contains 99 percent of all the mass in the solar system! Its gravity holds the whole system together.

Pluto

Not everyone is convinced that this hunk of icy rock is really a planet (and not just another Kuiper Belt Object). See page 38 for more on this!

Asteroid Belt

This is a region between Mars and Jupiter where lots of asteroids hang out. Asteroids are leftovers from the formation of the solar system. They're hunks of rock that never got pulled together to make a planet.

★ Astrotales

A New View

Long ago, people thought that Earth was at the center of the universe, and that the Sun and all the planets revolved around us! But about 2,300 years ago, a Greek astronomer named Aristarchus did some measurements and figured out that the Sun was much bigger than the Earth. With this new knowledge, he came up with the idea that the Sun should be at the center of everything. At the time, the idea was considered really crazy, so no one believed it.

Then in 1543—some 1,800 years later—a Polish astronomer named Copernicus presented this idea again, but with a lot of

Nicolaus Copernicus (1473–1543)

observations to back it up! This time, the idea didn't go away, and it became the starting point for a scientific revolution.

Who proved he was right? The stellar observations of Danish astronomer Tycho Brahe, the brilliant math of Johannes Kepler, and the physics of Isaac Newton brought it all together. That's how we got the view of the solar system you see above!

SIZE UP

If you could shrink the Sun to the size of a basketball, would the Earth be the size of a peppercorn, a coffee bean, or a walnut? And if you could squeeze the whole solar system into your living room, how far apart would all the planets be? Try this mission to get a handle on the planets and the distances between them!

Launch Objective

Size up and map out the planets of our solar system!

Your equipment

▶ **3 poppy seeds***
▶ **2 peppercorns***
▶ **2 coffee beans***
▶ **1 almond (in shell)***
▶ **1 walnut (in shell)***
▶ **1 basketball***
▶ **Team Universe cards from your first Space Case**
▶ **20-foot (6-m) piece of string**
▶ **Tape measure or ruler**
▶ **Black marker**

*Or something else the same size

Mission Procedure

Part 1: Mini-Planet Match Up!

1 Place the poppy seeds, the peppercorns, the coffee beans, the almond, the walnut, and the basketball on a table in front of you.

2 The basketball represents the Sun, and the other items represent the planets of our solar system. Each of the "planets" is just the right size in relation to the other planets and to the Sun. But which object is which planet? That's for you to figure out!

3 Place your Team Universe planet cards in a row: Mercury, Venus, Earth, Mars, Jupiter, Saturn, Uranus, Neptune, and then Pluto. Place the object that you think represents each planet on top of the corresponding card. (If you need more information to help you make your choices, skip ahead to Part 2 of this book!)

4 Check page 48 to see if you sized up the planets correctly!

Note:
The objects pictured above are shown in their actual sizes. If you're using another object instead, you can place it on top of the picture of the item you're replacing to make sure your object is the right size.

Mercury   Venus   Earth   Mars   Jupiter   Saturn   Uranus   Neptune   Pluto

THE SOLAR SYSTEM

Part 2: Go the Distance!

Now see how far apart the planets would be if you could shrink the solar system down to 20 feet (6 m)!

1 Place a 20-foot (6-m) piece of string on the floor. Place the Sun card from your Team Universe deck at one end of the string.

2 Now measure $2\frac{1}{4}$ inches (5.7 cm), and make a mark on the string with your black marker. Place your Mercury card below the black mark.

3 Now measure $4\frac{1}{2}$ inches (11.4 cm) from the end of the string and make another mark. Place your Venus card below the mark.

4 Keep placing planets along the string, using this chart to measure the distances:

Planet	Distance from Sun
Earth	6 inches (15 cm)
Mars	$9\frac{1}{4}$ inches (23.5 cm)
Jupiter	2 feet, 7 inches (79 cm)
Saturn	4 feet, 10 inches (1.5 m)
Uranus	9 feet, 9 inches (3 m)
Neptune	15 feet, 3 inches (4.6 m)
Pluto	20 feet (6 m)

5 Once you've placed your Pluto card at the very end of the string, step back and enjoy the view! (Of course, the planets aren't *really* lined up in a straight row. This view is just meant to show you how far apart their orbits are!)

Science, Please!

In Part 1, the objects that represented the planets were all just the right size in relation to each other. That means that your planet models were "to scale"—or, in other words, the models were all the same tiny fraction of the size of the real planets.

In Part 2, you created a *scale model* of the solar system. That means that all the distances between the planets were shrunk down by exactly the same amount.

What if you combined your planet models from Part 1 with the solar system model you made in Part 2? Well, in order to keep your size scale accurate, if you used the objects from Part 1, your solar system model would have to stretch as long as ten football fields!

That's why you used your Team Universe cards to stand in for planets in your 20-foot (6-m) solar system scale model. The planets would be really, really tiny in your model: Earth would be *microscopic*!

Part 2:
Tour the Planets!

Okay, cadet, now that you've seen how the solar system was formed, it's time to hop aboard the Space U Interplanetary Express and take the grand tour, from hot little Mercury to the chilly regions beyond Pluto, all in the space of twenty-seven pages!

Along the way, you'll visit lots of very different worlds—from the hazy yellow clouds of Venus, to the red rocks of Mars, to the orange, red, brown, and white swirls of Jupiter, to bright blue Neptune, and beyond. And you'll probably wonder...

Neptune

WHY ARE THE PLANETS ALL DIFFERENT COLORS?

Because they're made of different stuff! Even though the planets were all born in the same whirling cloud, they each got different types and amounts of gas and rock, depending on how big and how far away from the Sun they were. As the planets developed over time, these ingredients

Earth

Saturn

combined to form different substances—and these substances give the planets their colors.

Mars, for example, is known as the Red Planet because its rocky surface has lots of rusted iron in it (and if you've ever seen an old rusty can lying around, you know that rust looks red!). Your own planet looks mostly blue from space because water covers almost three-quarters of its surface.

The colors of the gas giants come from the gases that swirl around in their atmospheres. Neptune, for example, looks blue because its atmosphere has lots of a gas called *methane* in it, and methane reflects blue light. And how did Jupiter get its stripes? See page 30 to find out!

Jupiter

IT'S LIKE YOU'RE REALLY THERE!

What's an interplanetary tour without sightseeing stops? Not much! That's why you've been issued a 3-D Cosmic Viewer in this month's Space Case. With this handy little window into the solar system, you'll have plenty to *ooh* and *ahh* about!

So, grab your Cosmic Viewer (and your two discs), and let's get out of this world!

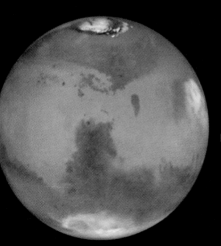

Mars

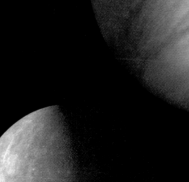

Mercury

Venus

MERCURY

W elcome to the first stop on your solar system tour, cadet:
Mercury, the planet of extremes! Better stay inside
your heat-shielded spacecraft, though, because this is no
place to wander around!

TO THE EXTREME!

During Mercury's long day (which lasts as long as *thirty* Earth
days!), the sunlit side of the planet gets *really* hot, with
temperatures reaching 800 degrees F (430 degrees C).
That's hot enough to melt parts of the rocky surface! But
then, when night falls, the temperature drops to –300
degrees F (–180 degrees C), and Mercury's surface hardens
into a jagged crust.

   Why does Mercury get so cold when it's so close to the Sun?
It's because Mercury has almost no atmosphere, so there's
not enough gas around it to hold on to the heat from the day.

SMASH HIT!

And you know what *else* happens to poor, unprotected
Mercury? Just like our Moon, it gets pounded by
meteorites that make huge craters on its surface.

   Most of the meteorite impacts happened billions of
years ago, when the solar system was still young (and
lots of rock was flying around!). *All* the inner planets
took quite a pounding back then. But unlike the other
inner planets, Mercury has no wind or rain or volcanic
activity to wipe away its craters, so they've stuck
around for ages!

MAKE WAY FOR MARINER AND MESSENGER

In the mid-1970s, the *Mariner 10* space probe made three passes by Mercury. The probe sent back images of half of Mercury's surface, showing us more detail than we'd ever seen before (try the Quick Blast below to see why Mercury is hard to observe from Earth!).

The next spacecraft to visit Mercury will be the *Messenger* probe, which is due to arrive at Mercury in 2007. The probe will use lots of different instruments to study Mercury's crust, magnetic field, and other features. Scientists hope they can use the information to understand Mercury's history!

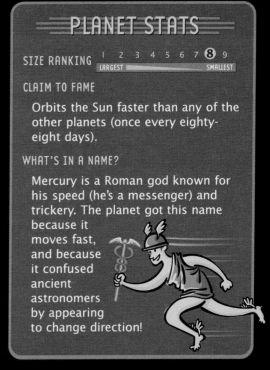

PLANET STATS

SIZE RANKING 1 2 3 4 5 6 7 **8** 9
LARGEST ▬▬▬ SMALLEST

CLAIM TO FAME

Orbits the Sun faster than any of the other planets (once every eighty-eight days).

WHAT'S IN A NAME?

Mercury is a Roman god known for his speed (he's a messenger) and trickery. The planet got this name because it moves fast, and because it confused ancient astronomers by appearing to change direction!

Mariner 10

QuickBlast

Disappearing Details

From Earth, the bright light of the Sun behind Mercury makes it tough for us to see Mercury's surface features. Try this Quick Blast to see why.

1 Turn on a lamp and angle it so the bulb faces you. You should be less than 3 feet (1 m) from the lamp.

2 Grab a pencil and study the details on it: words, chew marks, whatever.

3 Hold the pencil near the tip with the words or marks facing you. Stretch out your arm and hold the pencil at arm's length in front of the light bulb.

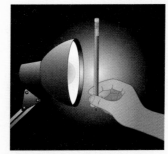

4 The words or teeth marks should be hard to see in front of the bright light bulb.

5 Now move the pencil slowly toward you, away from the lamp. You'll see how it becomes easier to read the words when the pencil gets farther from the light.

Mercury is way up close to the Sun—and just like it was hard to see the details on your pencil when it was close to the lamp, the bright Sun near Mercury makes it really hard for scientists to make out any of Mercury's details from here on Earth. That's why it's a *bright* idea to send probes like *Mariner 10* and *Messenger* to get a better view!

VENUS

Welcome to **Venus**, the next stop on your planetary tour. Unfortunately, "welcome" is not the right word here, because Venus is *not* a very welcoming place. It's hot (even hotter than *Mercury*), and it stinks like rotten eggs! Plus, there's acid rain, lots of lava-spewing volcanoes, and so much thick cloud cover that you'd never see any stars from the surface (if you could go there without getting cooked!).

So, long story short, cadet, you'd better just keep your spacecraft in orbit above this nasty planet—you'll enjoy Venus much more from afar!

WHY IS VENUS SUCH A HOT PLACE?

See all those yellow and brown swirls on Venus? Those are clouds. Really thick clouds. But they're not like Earth's clouds—they're made of different stuff. Our clouds are made of water vapor, but Venus's clouds are made of sulfuric acid (that's where the rotten-egg smell and the acid rain come from). Venus also has much more carbon dioxide in its atmosphere than we do—that's a gas that really holds on to heat!

So, with all those thick acid clouds and all that carbon dioxide, it's like Venus is wrapped in a super-heavy blanket. Heat gets trapped under the blanket, so Venus stays really, really hot—close to 900 degrees F (480 degrees C)! That's hot enough to melt metal! If Venus didn't have its thick blanket atmosphere, its surface temperature would only be around 140 degrees F (60 degrees C)!

PLANET STATS

SIZE RANKING 1 2 3 4 5 **6** 7 8 9
LARGEST — SMALLEST

CLAIM TO FAME

The hottest planet (and the stinkiest, too!).

WHAT'S IN A NAME?

Venus is the Roman goddess of love and beauty. The planet got this name because early astronomers thought it was very beautiful (it's the brightest planet we see in the night sky). Little did they know how nasty the place really is!

The space probe *Magellan*

OH, THE PRESSURE!

Besides the heat, Venus's thick atmosphere *also* means it has really strong air pressure.

Remember air pressure from your first month at Space U? Remember how you pumped some of the air out of your Space Simulator and watched the marshmallow get bigger? And then when you let the air back in, the air pressed the marshmallow down to a small, shriveled lump?

Well, the air pressure on Venus is extra, extra, *extra* strong! It's *ninety* times stronger than the air pressure on Earth at surface level. The pressure is so powerful that your body would be crushed by it! Yikes!

VISITORS TO VENUS: BEWARE!

Because of the heat and pressure, there haven't been many space probes that have managed to land on Venus's surface. Most of them are quickly melted or crushed.

To see Venus's surface, we've sent space probes like *Magellan* to orbit around Venus and peek through the clouds. How did *Magellan* do it? With radar! That means *Magellan* beamed down radio waves and timed how long it took for them to hit the surface and bounce back. With this information, scientists could figure out the shape of Venus's surface. To find out more about this planet-mapping technique, turn the page and try the next mission!

COSMIC VIEWER

DISC 1, IMAGE 1

Grab your Cosmic Viewer—it's time for some sightseeing! Insert Disc 1 and turn it so that the caption for Image 1 is in the caption space. Enjoy the view!

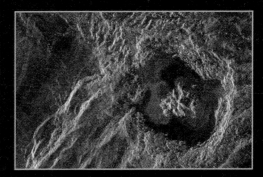

This 22-mile (34-km) wide crater on Venus was caused by a big asteroid that smashed into the planet's surface. The image was created by the *Magellan* space probe, which mapped out 99 percent of Venus's surface using radar.

RADAR

When a planet is too hostile for landing (like Venus), what's a space explorer to do? Explore it with radar, like the space probe *Magellan* did! Try this mission to see how radar works on your very own shoebox planet!

Launch Objective

▷ **Probe a hidden planetary surface and draw a map of it, without ever seeing it with your eyes!**

Your equipment

▷ **Shoebox with a lid**
▷ **Scissors**
▷ **Ruler**
▷ **Pencil or pen**
▷ **A few small stones, boxes, blocks, and other objects**
▷ **Tape**
▷ **Radar Log pages from the Space University web site**

Personnel

▷ **A friend**
▷ **An IGA (Intergalactic Adult)**

Mission Procedure

Part 1: Design a Planet Landscape

1 Remove the shoebox lid and turn the shoebox on its side.

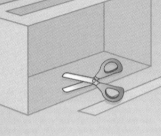

2 Have an IGA help you cut a slit the width of your ruler along the top side of the box, running from one end to the other.

3 Lay your ruler next to the slit and mark off a small line every 1 inch (2.5 cm). Number the lines from left to right.

4 Now, leave the room while your friend creates a planet landscape on the bottom side of the box, directly below the slit. Your friend can use rocks and other objects to create small hills and large mountains. Make sure the objects are all taped down so your planet's surface stays in place!

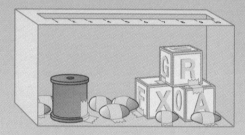

5 Once the landscape is complete, your friend should use the shoebox's lid to cover the open side of the shoebox, then call you back into the room to explore this new planet's landscape!

Part 2: Explore Your Planet

To explore your shoebox planet, you'll need the Radar Log pages from the Space U web site (www.scholastic.com/space). Jump on-line to print them out! Or, if you prefer, you can just make a graph like the one below.

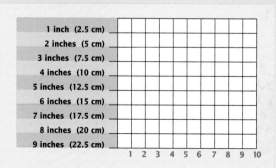

	1	2	3	4	5	6	7	8	9	10
1 inch (2.5 cm)										
2 inches (5 cm)										
3 inches (7.5 cm)										
4 inches (10 cm)										
5 inches (12.5 cm)										
6 inches (15 cm)										
7 inches (17.5 cm)										
8 inches (20 cm)										
9 inches (22.5 cm)										

RULER

1 Starting at mark #1 on the shoebox's slit, slide your ruler down into the box and see how far it goes until it touches the planet's surface. Make sure not to push the ruler too hard—stop as soon as it touches something!

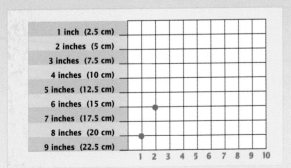

2 Look at your ruler to find the distance from the top of the box to the planet's surface. Mark that distance on your Radar Log above mark #1.

3 At each of the other marks along the slit, slide your ruler down and record the distance on your Radar Log.

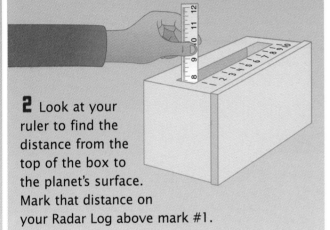

	1	2	3	4	5	6	7	8	9	10
1 inch (2.5 cm)										
2 inches (5 cm)										
3 inches (7.5 cm)										
4 inches (10 cm)										
5 inches (12.5 cm)										
6 inches (15 cm)		●								
7 inches (17.5 cm)										
8 inches (20 cm)	●									
9 inches (22.5 cm)										

4 Now connect the dots on your Radar Log. You should get a line that shows peaks and valleys, as if you were looking at the landscape from a distance.

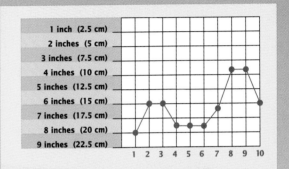

5 Remove the shoebox's lid. Does your landscape sketch match up to the actual landscape of your shoebox planet? Congratulations, cadet! You've just mapped out a planet without ever setting eyes on it!

Science, Please!

Space probes like *Magellan* map out a planet using a process very similar to the one you used in this mission. The probe orbits a planet and beams radio waves down to the surface. Then the probe measures how long it takes for the waves to bounce back. If the waves hit something high like a mountaintop, they'll bounce back more quickly because they have a shorter distance to travel.

You used a similar technique in this mission— you measured the distance you could extend your ruler into the box before it hit the planet's surface. You might have noticed that the landscape sketch you got looked *sort of* like the real thing, but not exactly. That's because you were only taking a measurement once every inch (or 2.5 cm). If you took more measurements, you'd get a more exact landscape.

EARTH

After traveling past two sweltering, unwelcoming planets, you're probably looking for a place where you can touchdown for a rest stop! Fortunately, Earth is the next planet on your solar system tour, so you'll feel right at home!

THE SWEET SPOT

One of the reasons you feel so comfy on Earth is that it's just the right distance from the Sun. Earth is not too close to the Sun (like sweltering Mercury or Venus) or too far away (like chilly Mars, or the even colder planets beyond). As scientists say, Earth is in the "life zone" of our Sun—that is, the distance from the Sun where the temperatures are just right for life to exist.

THE PLACE TO GO FOR H_2O

Earth's nice temperatures allow water to exist in a liquid state, which means that living things can survive. Mars might have been a wet planet once, but now it only has water vapor and ice. Lucky for us, more than 70 percent of Earth's surface is still covered by liquid water—which makes this planet a great place to call home.

THE AIR WE SHARE

Earth also has an atmosphere that gives us the air we breathe. Our atmosphere is made up of a mixture of gases—like nitrogen, oxygen, and carbon dioxide. Besides letting us breathe, our atmosphere protects us from the Sun's harsh radiation and from hunks of space rock that fly toward our planet.

Of course, other planets have atmospheres, too. What makes *ours* just right for life? Try the next mission to find out!

PLANET STATS

SIZE RANKING 1 2 3 4 **5** 6 7 8 9
LARGEST ———————————— SMALLEST

CLAIM TO FAME
The only planet in our solar system known to harbor life.

WHAT'S IN A NAME?
The name Earth is related to the German word "erda" and the Dutch word "aerde," which both mean soil, or earth.

EARTH IS JUST RIGHT!

What is it about our home planet that keeps the temperature just right for us Earthlings? Try this mission to find out (and melt some butter for your popcorn while you're at it!).

Launch Objective

Simulate the conditions on Mercury, Venus, and Earth to see how Earth keeps its climate just right!

Your equipment

▶ **Pat of butter**
▶ **Butter knife**
▶ **2 plastic bags with zip closures**
▶ **Scissors**
▶ **Paper plate**
▶ **Desk lamp**

Mission Procedure

1 Cut the pat of butter into three equal pieces.

2 Snip off the corner of one of the plastic bags and put one piece of butter inside the corner. Place this piece of butter on the paper plate underneath the turned-off lamp, making sure that the bag covers the top of the butter and the bag's opening faces away from the lamp. This piece of butter represents planet Earth.

3 Place the second piece of butter inside the second plastic bag. Seal the bag and put it under the lamp next to "Earth." This is Venus.

4 Place the third piece of butter on the plate next to the other two, with no bag at all. This is Mercury!

5 Now turn on the lamp and position the bulb about 6 inches (15 cm) above

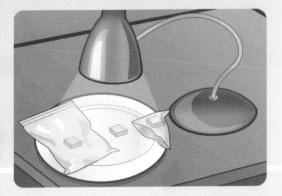

the paper plate. Make sure all the butter pieces are the same distance from the lamp.

6 Watch the three pieces of butter for about ten minutes. Which one melts first? Which melts second? And which piece of butter stays solid the longest?

Science, Please!

The butter inside the sealed plastic bag (Venus) should have been the first to melt. That's because the plastic bag captured the heat from the lamp and hung on to it, making the temperature inside the bag go up. Venus's thick atmosphere acts the same way—it won't let heat escape, so Venus gets sweltering hot!

The butter with no bag (Mercury) should have been the *second* to melt. Mercury gets very hot because it has little atmosphere to protect it from the Sun—but it doesn't get as hot as Venus, as you saw in this mission.

The butter in the open bag (Earth) should have stayed solid the longest. This is because the plastic protected the butter from *some* of the lamp's heat, while the open side of the bag allowed the heat that *did* get in to escape (unlike on "Venus," where that heat stayed trapped). Our atmosphere works in a similar way—it protects us from *some* of the Sun's rays, but it also allows some heat to escape. It's not too smothering like Venus's atmosphere, and it's not too weak like Mercury's. It's just right!

MARS

It's red, it's rocky, and it's right next door! Welcome to **Mars**, cadet—where the days are freezing, the nights are even colder, and the mountains and valleys are out of this world!

Get geared up for landing, because you can actually park your spacecraft on this planet and take a walk around! Just make sure you've got the right space suit to protect you from the harsh conditions!

UNDER THE WEATHER

During the day, Mars is a chilly place—only about 32 degrees F (0 degrees C) at the equator, which is like winter on Earth. At night, Mars's thin atmosphere can't hold on to the little heat Mars gets from the Sun—so the planet cools down to –80 degrees F (–60 degrees C). Brrrr!

You'll have to bundle up to stay warm, but at least you won't have to pack a raincoat—because there's no wet weather in the forecast here! Most of the water on Mars is frozen in the soil and in the ice caps on the north and south poles.

Without liquid water, life as we know it can't survive. But it's possible that Mars was once a very wet place—so we're still searching for signs of Martian life!

MISSION TO MARS

Scientists are bursting with questions about Mars, especially because of the possibility for life, so NASA has launched lots of probes to check out the Red Planet. The first were *Mariner 4, 6,* and *7*, which flew by Mars in the 1960s and sent back pictures and information about the planet's surface and atmosphere.

The next missions that NASA sent to Mars were *Viking 1* and *2*, in 1975. These spacecraft carried the first probes ever to land on the Red Planet! The landers searched for evidence of life on Mars—but didn't find any.

Later missions included the *Mars Global Surveyor*, which was sent to orbit Mars in 1996, and *Mars Pathfinder*, which landed on the Martian surface the same year. Use your Cosmic Viewer to check out some of the cool images that these spacecraft beamed back to Earth!

PLANET STATS

SIZE RANKING

1	2	3	4	5	6	**7**	8	9
LARGEST								SMALLEST

CLAIM TO FAME

This planet has the biggest volcano and the longest canyon in the solar system!

WHAT'S IN A NAME?

Mars is the Roman god of war, which relates to the planet's reddish color.

MARTIAN MOONS

Two strange little moons, Phobos and Deimos, go 'round the Red Planet. They're most likely asteroids that were pulled in by Mars's gravity. Deimos is covered in huge craters, and Phobos looks like a potato!

Mars's moon Phobos

COSMIC VIEWER

DISC 1, IMAGES 2-6

Insert Disc 1 into your Cosmic Viewer to see five great views of the Red Planet!

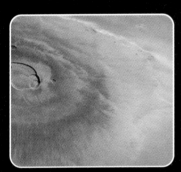

IMAGE 2

Here's Olympus Mons, the biggest mountain on Mars (it's actually an extinct volcano). Olympus Mons is taller than three Mount Everests and about as wide as the entire Hawaiian Island chain. In fact, it's the largest volcano in the solar system! This photo and the next one were taken by the *Mars Global Surveyor*.

IMAGE 3

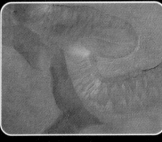

The valleys you can see in this image sure look like dried-up riverbeds, don't they? If this is the case, it could mean that water used to flow on Mars.

IMAGE 4

This photo was taken by the *Mars Pathfinder* lander, which touched down on Mars in 1997. The two hills on the horizon have been named the Twin Peaks. Even though they look tall and far away, they're actually small and nearby. It would take just ten or fifteen minutes to walk to the nearest one!

IMAGE 5

Here's another section of the Martian landscape that was photographed on the *Mars Pathfinder* mission. It's possible that all the rocks you see were carried here by a gigantic flood!

IMAGE 6

Here you can see the *Sojourner* rover, a solar-powered vehicle about the size of a microwave oven. At the bottom left is the ramp that the rover used to get from the *Pathfinder* lander to the surface of Mars. *Sojourner* studied the rocks and soil of Mars and sent information and photos back to Earth.

MARS MATCH UP

Ready to explore Mars for yourself? Then take a look at these Martian snapshots and see if you can figure out what you're seeing! Most of these images were taken by the *Mars Global Surveyor* (launched in 1996), but image B was created with pictures from the *Viking* probes (launched in 1975).

Launch Objective

Name that Martian surface feature!

Your equipment

▶ Just your eyes!

Mission Procedure

Look at the images on these pages and see if you can match each one with one of the following descriptions. You can check your answers on page 48!

1 These layers of rock have been worn away by the wind.

2 Martian wind created these dusty sand dunes.

3 The frost on these sand dunes is beginning to melt after a Martian winter.

4 This is Valles Marineris, the longest and deepest canyon in the solar system.

5 Frozen carbon dioxide at Mars's south pole creates these patterns.

6 This canyon could be a riverbed that once held water!

7 From above, this hill looks like a pyramid or a star.

8 Some think this surface feature looks like a face when seen from above!

9 This round crater was created by an asteroid that crashed onto Mars.

10 This ancient volcano could be as tall as 3 miles (5 km) high.

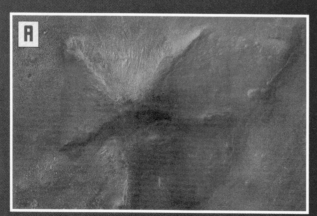

A

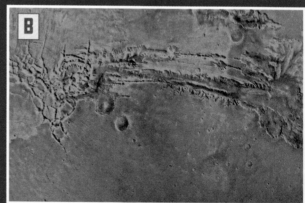

B

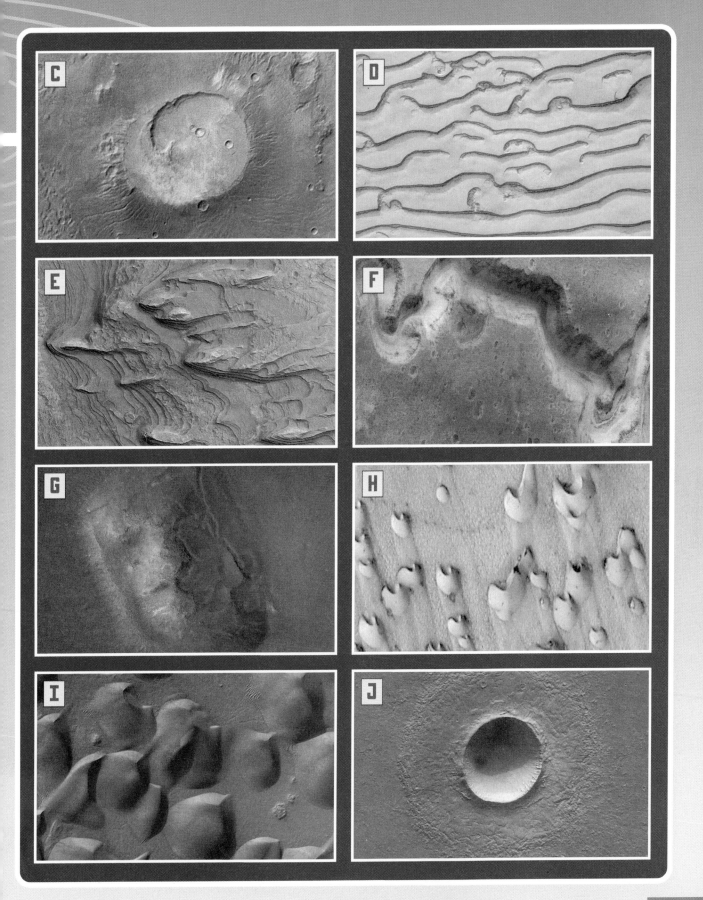

THE ASTEROID

The trip from Mars to Jupiter is a long haul, cadet—I hope you brought a couple hundred books to read! But before we get anywhere near Jupiter, we have a rocky road ahead: the asteroid belt!

This region of the solar system contains millions of giant rocks called *asteroids*, each orbiting the Sun on its own path. These asteroids come in all different shapes and sizes (the largest, called Ceres, is 570 miles [914 km] across!). And although they're usually referred to as "rocks," asteroids are sometimes made of metal, too.

PLANET FAILURE

Scientists think that these asteroids are the makings of a small planet that never managed to form the way the others in our solar system did—these rocks just never clumped together into one big ball. Why not? Probably because the strong gravity of nearby Jupiter pulled on the rocks and caused such a stir that they could never "get it together"!

COSMIC VIEWER

DISC 1, IMAGE 7

Want to see an asteroid that actually has a moon? Then insert Disc 1 and turn to Image 7 and check it out!

The asteroid Ida has a little moon of its own named Dactyl, which orbits Ida just like our Moon orbits the Earth. Dactyl, which is only about a mile (1.5 km) wide, was the first asteroid moon ever discovered!

NEAR-EARTH ASTEROIDS

Some asteroids have orbits that bring them close to Earth—they're called "Near-Earth Asteroids," or NEAs. To be considered an NEA, an asteroid has to come within 121 million miles (193 million km) of Earth. That's farther out than Mars, but it's still considered "near" in space terms! Scientists keep track of these asteroids so they'll know when one might be on a collision course with our planet.

BELT

An asteroid impact could be *very* devastating—just ask a dinosaur! (Many scientists believe that the dinosaurs were wiped out by the effects of a giant asteroid impact.) But nowadays, with advance warning from astronomers, we could destroy or redirect an asteroid that was threatening to plow into our planet. Too bad the dinosaurs didn't have an *astronomerosaurus* to save them!

FLASH FACT

The word "asteroid" comes from Greek and means "star-like." It was first used in 1802 by astronomer William Herschel (who also discovered Uranus) to describe the points of light he saw with his telescope that he knew weren't stars, planets, or comets.

QuickBlast

Spot the Dot

How do astronomers discover asteroids? By looking at pictures just like the ones you see below. Do you think you can spot the asteroid?

1 Compare the image on the left with the image on the right. Both are photos of the night sky (but the white and black colors are reversed to make the images easier to study). The photos were taken sixteen minutes apart.

Most of the dots are stars, which you'll see in the same position in both images. But *one* of the dots *changes* positions. Can you spot the dot that moved? That's your asteroid! It moves in relation to the stars because it's traveling around the Sun.

2 Check page 48 to see if you spotted the right dot! And in case you're wondering, this asteroid was discovered in the year 2000—it's called asteroid 2000 QW7.

3 Visit this month's Space U web site (www.scholastic.com/space) for more asteroid-spotting fun!

JUPITER

You'll be able to spot Jupiter in the distance long before you arrive—because this planet is enormous! Jupiter contains more matter than all of the other planets *plus* the asteroids combined. You could stuff 1,300 Earths into this giant planet!

This is the first of the gas giants you'll visit on your interplanetary tour. Like the others—Saturn, Uranus, and Neptune—this planet has a relatively small rocky core surrounded by layers of liquid and gas (mostly hydrogen and helium, in Jupiter's case).

Just don't expect to land on this striped giant! If you tried to go down into the atmosphere, you'd find yourself squashed by the extremely high pressure!

A DAY THAT'S OVER IN A FLASH

Jupiter has the shortest day of all the planets—just ten hours! That's because the planet has a spinning speed of up to 26,000 miles per hour (48,000 km/h). This super-fast whirling makes Jupiter's winds howl at up to 400 miles per hour (650 km/h)!

Jupiter's famous Great Red Spot is a storm that's been brewing for at least 300 years! It's about twice the size of Earth.

HOW DID JUPITER GET ITS STRIPES?

With its orange, brown, and white stripes, Jupiter looks sort of like a cosmic tiger. But the bands of color on Jupiter are actually streaks of gases whirling at high speeds. The lighter bands are created by ices high in the atmosphere, while the darker bands are deeper down. The colors come from different substances mixed in with the gases, like sulfur and phosphorous.

GALILEO'S MOONS

In 1610, astronomer Galileo Galilei peered at Jupiter through a telescope and found mysterious points of light surrounding the planet. Over several nights, Galileo continued to look at the lights, making sketches of their positions. He soon realized that these lights were *moons* (Jupiter's four largest, Ganymede, Io, Callisto, and Europa!).

PLANET STATS

SIZE RANKING **1** 2 3 4 5 6 7 8 9
LARGEST ▬▬▬▬▬ SMALLEST

CLAIM TO FAME
The biggest planet in our solar system!

WHAT'S IN A NAME?
Jupiter is named for the Roman king of the gods, since it's the giant of the solar system.

Nowadays, we know that Jupiter has more than sixty moons in orbit around it, creating what some people call a "mini solar system." Most of these moons are asteroids that got pulled in by Jupiter's strong gravity.

MODERN-DAY GALILEO

The first spacecraft to orbit Jupiter was named *Galileo* after the great astronomer. *Galileo* arrived at Jupiter in 1995 and stayed in orbit until 2003. During that time, it sent thousands of images back to Earth and helped scientists learn lots about Jupiter's atmosphere and moons.

Galileo orbiting Jupiter

DISC 2, IMAGES 1-3

Grab your Cosmic Viewer and get ready for your own mission to Jupiter! Insert Disc 2 to take a look at three of the giant planet's biggest moons.

IMAGE 1

Here, Jupiter's moon Io passes in front of the giant planet. Io appears close to Jupiter in this picture, but in fact, you could fit two and a half Jupiters between Io and the clouds behind it! Io is a hot and wretched place—it's famous for its many active volcanoes.

IMAGE 2

In this picture, Jupiter looms in the distance behind its moon Europa. Europa has an icy surface that's covered with cracks. Based on information sent back by the probe *Galileo*, it's suspected that a liquid ocean lies beneath the ice. Some think we might find living creatures there!

IMAGE 3

Here's Jupiter (in the distance) with Ganymede, its biggest moon. Ganymede is the largest moon in the whole solar system—it's bigger than the planets Pluto and Mercury!

N ow that you've passed your first gas giant, cadet, you probably know what to expect when you arrive at Saturn. Yep, just like Jupiter, there's no sense trying to land your spacecraft here, because there's no place to touchdown! Like the other gas giants, Saturn is mostly gas with a relatively small rock core (about the size of one of the inner planets).

WINDY WORLD

It's also *really* blustery inside Saturn's thick atmosphere—the winds can whip up to a rate of 1,400 miles per hour (2,250 km/h)! That's ten times stronger than hurricane winds on Earth! These high-speed winds create the bands of gold and brown you see on the planet.

A PLANET WITH EARS?

Galileo first saw Saturn's rings in 1610, but through his low-powered telescope, the rings looked like ears bulging from the planet's sides. Amazed, he concluded that Saturn had two sister planets attached to its middle. In 1655, Dutch astronomer Christiaan Huygens had a telescope large enough to see that the bulges were really a set of rings.

RING AROUND THE PLANET

Saturn's famous rings might *look* solid, but they actually consist of billions of ice chunks racing around the planet in orderly rows. Some of these chunks are as tiny as golf balls and others are as big as football stadiums!

PLANET STATS

SIZE RANKING 1 **2** 3 4 5 6 7 8 9
LARGEST ▬▬▬▬▬ SMALLEST

CLAIM TO FAME
This planet is famous for its large set of beautiful rings.

WHAT'S IN A NAME?
Ancient astronomers named slow-moving Saturn after a Roman god of agriculture.

Saturn's rings are more than twice as wide as the planet itself, but they're not as thick as you might think. They're only about as tall as a 50-story building!

In 1676, astronomer Gian Dominico Cassini discovered a gap in Saturn's rings. Today we call it the Cassini Division. Turn to page 35 to find out about the spacecraft named after Cassini and its mission to Saturn!

The Cassini Division, a gap in Saturn's rings nearly 3,000 miles (5,000 km) wide

MANY, MANY MOONS

You would think that beautiful rings would be enough for one planet, but Saturn's charms also include many moons— thirty and counting! The largest, Titan, is one of the only moons in the solar system with an atmosphere! Its atmosphere is mostly nitrogen, which means it might resemble the atmosphere Earth had in its early years.

Titan, Saturn's largest moon

COSMIC VIEWER

DISC 2, IMAGE 4

Grab your Cosmic Viewer to see Saturn in three amazing dimensions!

Here you can see three of Saturn's moons (the pale dots below the planet). See the dark spot on Saturn, just beneath the rings? That's a shadow cast by one of the moons. You can also see the shadow cast by the planet against the rings in the back (it looks like a chunk taken out of the rings on the right side).

SATURN FLOATS!

If you could find a swimming pool large enough, Saturn would float! Really! All the other planets, on the other hand, would sink to the bottom of the pool. What's the difference? It all has to do with *density*—the measurement of how much mass (or "stuff") is squeezed into a space.

Launch Objective

▶ **Compare the densities of marbles, marshmallows, and more!**

Your equipment

▶ **A clear glass or jar**
▶ **Pancake syrup**
▶ **Vegetable oil**
▶ **Water**
▶ **Small objects of different sizes and weights (like marshmallows, marbles, small rocks, coins, grapes, corks, or coffee beans)**

Mission Procedure

1 Pour a $1\frac{1}{2}$-inch (4-cm) layer of pancake syrup into the glass.

2 Slowly pour a $1\frac{1}{2}$-inch (4-cm) layer of oil on top of the syrup.

3 Pour a $1\frac{1}{2}$-inch (4-cm) layer of water into the glass.

4 Wait for the liquids to separate and settle into layers. Notice which liquid ends up on the bottom, in the middle, and on top.

5 Now drop a marble or a small rock into the glass. Where does it end up?

6 Drop in a different object, like a grape or a peanut. Which layer does it settle in? Keep dropping in objects and watch where they settle. Why do you think the objects end up in different layers?

Science, Please!

In this mission, you compared the densities of different materials. Remember, density is the measurement of how much mass is packed into a space. If an object has a lot of mass in a little space, it has a *high* density—like a metal coin or a rock. If an object has *less* mass packed into it, it has a *low* density—like a marshmallow or a cork. If you put items of different densities together, they'll tend to arrange themselves so that the high-density items are on the bottom and the low-density items are on top.

The three liquids settled into different layers because they have different densities. The oil has the lowest density—that's why it ended up on top. The syrup has the highest density, so it sat on the bottom.

When you dropped an object into the glass, you saw how the object's density compared to the density of each liquid. Objects that fell to the bottom of the glass won the prize for highest density. Objects that floated on top of the oil had the lowest density. If an object ended up *between* two layers, it had a density between those two liquids.

Among the planets, Saturn wins the prize for lowest density—it's the only planet that would float on water! The other planets are made of much denser stuff!

Dr. Linda Spilker

CASSINI SCIENTIST

Cassini was the astronomer who discovered a gap in Saturn's rings, so it makes sense that a spacecraft designed to explore the rings in detail would be named after him. We caught up with *Cassini* Deputy Project Scientist Linda Spilker at NASA's Jet Propulsion Laboratory to get the scoop on this spacecraft, which plans to hang out with Saturn from 2004 through 2008 (and possibly beyond!).

Question: So what's *Cassini*'s game plan?

Answer: First we'll fly by Saturn's moon Phoebe. It's probably a captured object (like an asteroid) and might look quite different from other moons. Then we'll go orbit around Saturn for a while and visit some of its other moons.

Q: What will you investigate on the moons?

A: Well, a robotic probe is going to visit the surface of Titan, Saturn's largest moon. Titan's surface is covered with smog, so we don't know if there's solid ground or a liquid ocean below. The probe was made to float just in case. Titan seems to be a lot like Earth. We don't think there's life there, but if there is, it might help us understand how life started on Earth.

Q: How will you investigate Saturn's rings?

A: We'll fly within a few tens of thousands of kilometers of the rings. That's the closest any spacecraft has gotten to them. The three main rings are like three different labs to test ideas. We're also going to look at how Saturn's moons interact with the rings.

Q: Which part of the mission is your specialty?

A: I look at the temperature of the ring particles to see what they're made of—icy spheres or fluffy snowballs.

Q: How long will *Cassini* stay at Saturn?

A: The whole mission is scheduled to last until July 2008, but we have enough fuel to last six years total. Then we'll probably burn the spacecraft in Saturn's atmosphere so it doesn't crash into a moon. That way we can study Saturn's atmosphere, too.

Dr. Spilker standing in front of the *Cassini* spacecraft

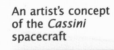

An artist's concept of the *Cassini* spacecraft

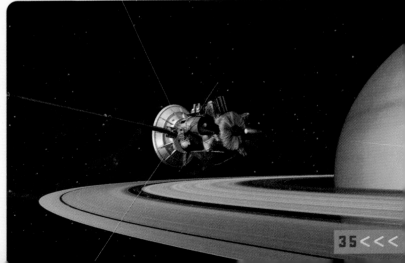

URANUS

The next planet on your tour seems kind of boring at first glance. **Uranus** looks completely blue-gray—that's because of a gas in its upper atmosphere called methane, which reflects blue light. Clouds of frozen methane crystals cover the planet and hide any storms or stripes that might lie beneath, which makes for a pretty plain planet.

But hold on! If you can make out Uranus's faint rings, you'll notice they're going up and down, instead of side to side like the rings of Saturn. Why do they go up and down? Because Uranus spins on its side! Scientists think the planet started out upright and was knocked sideways when an Earth-sized object smashed into it.

THE VIEW FROM VOYAGER

The first (and only!) spacecraft to visit Uranus was *Voyager 2*, which passed by in 1986. The probe flew straight through Uranus's rings, discovered two new rings, and caught glimpses of ten small moons never seen before!

PLANET GEORGE?

Believe it or not, Uranus was originally called George! On March 13, 1781, astronomer William Herschel was making a star map when he came across a strange object. At first, Herschel thought it was a distant comet, but after much debate, astronomers realized it was a planet. Herschel named the planet in honor of England's King George III. But Herschel's astronomer buddies wanted the planet's name to fit in with the mythical theme of the other planet names. After Herschel died in 1822, they renamed the planet Uranus.

PLANET STATS

SIZE RANKING   1 2 **3** 4 5 6 7 8 9
LARGEST ————————————— SMALLEST

CLAIM TO FAME
This planet rolls around the Sun on its side!

WHAT'S IN A NAME?
According to Greek mythology, Uranus is the father of the Sun. Astronomer Johannes Bode suggested the name to match the other planets, which were named after gods from Greek and Roman mythology.

COSMIC VIEWER

DISC 2, IMAGE 5

Take a peek at Uranus and one of its moons!

Here you can see Uranus in the distance behind its moon Ariel, which has large valleys and canyons stretching across its surface. Ariel, like many of Uranus's moons, is named after a character in a Shakespearean play.

NEPTUNE

Next on your tour is **Neptune**! At first you'll notice that this planet looks a lot like Uranus—they're about the same size and they're both shades of blue. But Neptune is a whole *lot* bluer than Uranus—and it's got spots!

A CLOSER LOOK

Neptune's a brighter blue because it has *more* methane in its upper atmosphere to reflect blue light. Not only that, but the methane on Neptune looks different because it's in gas form, not frozen like on Uranus. That's because Neptune is a warmer planet, even though it's farther from the Sun—it radiates heat from inside. Wisps of frozen methane crystals sometimes float across Neptune's atmosphere, creating pale clouds.

FRECKLE FACE

With stormy winds of 1,300 miles per hour (2,000 km/h) churning its clouds, Neptune is the windiest place in the solar system! One of Neptune's giant storms, the Great Dark Spot, was like a big blue mole on its face. But unlike Jupiter's Great Red Spot (which has been around for at least 300 years), the blemish on Neptune lasted only a few years. Now we know that stormy spots appear and disappear on Neptune all the time.

THE HUNT FOR THE MYSTERY PLANET

Neptune was first discovered in 1846, but astronomers knew it was there years before then, because something seemed to be pulling Uranus off course. After doing a lot of math, some astronomers proposed that another planet's gravity was tugging on Uranus. They began to search for the culprit, and soon, a race to find the new planet had begun. It was German astronomer Johann Galle who finally discovered Neptune in 1846.

PLANET STATS

SIZE RANKING 1 2 3 **④** 5 6 7 8 9
LARGEST ▬▬▬▬▬▬ SMALLEST

CLAIM TO FAME
The windiest planet in the solar system!

WHAT'S IN A NAME?
Neptune is the Roman god of the sea. Astronomers chose the name because the planet is the color of Earth's oceans.

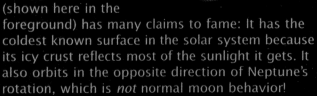

COSMIC VIEWER

DISC 2, IMAGE 6

Catch a glimpse of Triton, Neptune's super-chilly moon!

Triton, the largest of Neptune's eight moons, is bigger than Pluto! Triton (shown here in the foreground) has many claims to fame: It has the coldest known surface in the solar system because its icy crust reflects most of the sunlight it gets. It also orbits in the opposite direction of Neptune's rotation, which is *not* normal moon behavior!

Pluto's moon Charon is about half Pluto's size—that's quite a hefty moon!

PLUTO

After your trip past four gas giants, **Pluto** might come as a surprise. First of all, Pluto is no giant—it's even smaller than our Moon. And second, Pluto's not gassy—it's just a ball of rock and ice.

Pluto also has a weird orbit—it travels around the Sun at an angle compared to the other planets, and it moves inside Neptune's orbit for 20 of the 248 years it takes to orbit the Sun. This means that Neptune is sometimes even farther from the Sun than Pluto!

This illustration shows you how we *think* Pluto looks. We haven't been able to see it up-close because Pluto has never been visited by a probe. But stay tuned—NASA is planning a mission called *New Horizons* that aims to reach Pluto in 2015.

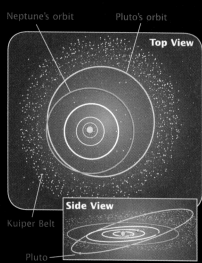

Neptune's orbit   Pluto's orbit

Top View

Side View

Kuiper Belt

Pluto

JUST ANOTHER FROZEN ROCK?

Because it's such an oddball, some astronomers think Pluto shouldn't even be considered a planet. They think it's part of the Kuiper Belt, a region of ice and rock out past Neptune. Pluto is very much like the icy hunks found in this region—it's just a lot bigger.

So, cadet, is Pluto the smallest planet in our solar system, or is it the king of the Kuiper Belt? Read more about this raging debate on the next page, then stop by the Space U web site (www.scholastic.com/space) to cast your vote! You'll find the Pluto Poll on this month's bulletin board.

PLANET STATS

SIZE RANKING 1 2 3 4 5 6 7 8 **9**
LARGEST ———————— SMALLEST

CLAIM TO FAME
It's the smallest, most distant planet. It's also the most *controversial* one, because some say we shouldn't even call it a planet!

WHAT'S IN A NAME?
Pluto is the Roman god of the underworld; the name seems to fit the planet in the darkest reaches of the solar system.

Dr. Neil deGrasse Tyson

ASTROPHYSICIST

Meet one astrophysicist who firmly believes that Pluto should *not* be called a planet—despite the piles of letters he gets in protest! Dr. Neil deGrasse Tyson directs the Hayden Planetarium at the Rose Center for Earth and Space in New York City.

(right) At the Rose Center for Earth and Space, the solar system display shows only eight planets—Pluto is not among them.

Question: There are all sorts of different objects orbiting the Sun. We call some of them planets. What's a planet, anyway?

Answer: The word "planet" has no scientifically agreed-upon definition. It's confusing. "Planet" had clear meaning in the days of the ancient Greeks, who saw seven "wanderers" against the background of stars (the word "planet" comes from the Greek word for "wanderer"). No disagreements, given the clean and clear definition.

Q: Is Pluto a planet?

A: Not according to our exhibits at the Rose Center. We no longer use the term "planet." Instead we've organized the solar system into families of similar objects. But according to the International Astronomical Union, Pluto is officially a planet. Their decision is based more on culture, history, and tradition than on science.

Q: Why was Pluto originally called a planet in 1930?

A: Astronomers expected Pluto to be the size of Uranus or Neptune. But instead, we learned in the 1970s that Pluto was smaller than Earth's Moon.

Q: When did some astronomers change their minds about Pluto?

A: Since the 1970s, everyone knew that Pluto was different. When the first Kuiper Belt Object was discovered in 1992, we put Pluto into that category. This discovery started the transition.

Q: Are there other things that used to be called planets but were "downgraded"?

A: Yes, in the early 1800s the first asteroids were originally called planets. Then we learned how small they are and how many there are. Forty years later they were all reclassified as new kinds of objects in the solar system called asteroids.

Q: What do people say when they write you letters to protest your view?

A: In nearly all cases, if you sift through the words, you find layers of emotion, nostalgia and, simply, *love* for this tiny object.

MOON

Congrats, cadet—you've zipped by all the planets in our solar system, and you checked out a bunch of really cool moons along the way. Now you're ready to proceed to the outer reaches of our solar system. But wait! Do you remember whose moon is whose? Better do a quick review!

Launch Objective

> Match the moons with their planets!

Your equipment

▶ Your space smarts

Mission Procedure

See if you can match the moons shown here with the planets they orbit (listed below). You can check your answers on page 48!

1 **Mars**
2 **Jupiter**
3 **Saturn**
4 **Uranus**
5 **Neptune**

Size Wise

The moons shown here are to *scale*, which means they're just the right sizes in relation to each other. Here's how big *our* Moon would be compared to these other moons.

Titan ▼

Between Titan and the planet it orbits there are more than a dozen other moons, plus a vast set of rings. Titan is one of the only moons with an atmosphere, which might be similar to the atmosphere on Earth billions of years ago. Titan might also have lakes and oceans, but filled with super-cold natural gas instead of water!

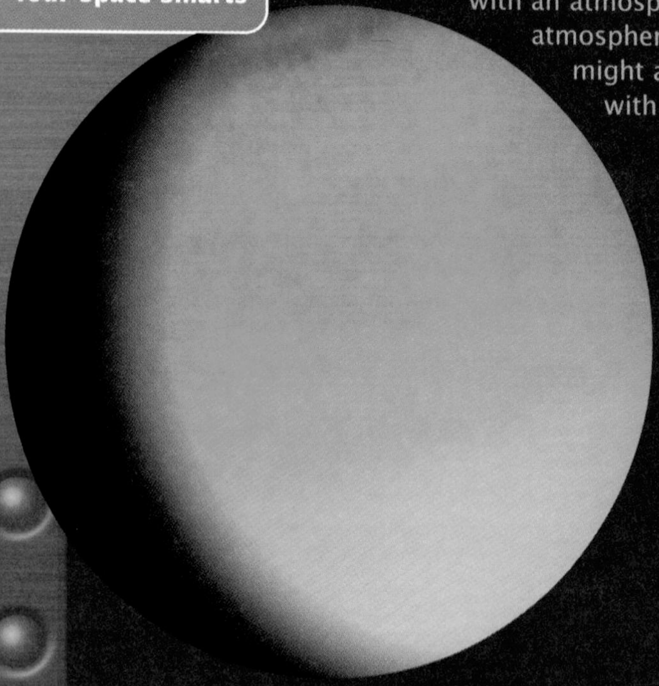

Triton ▶

This far-out moon has the coldest surface temperature of all the planets and moons our probes have visited. Triton has volcanoes that spew icy lava and geysers that spray liquid nitrogen and dust several miles into space!

Phobos ▶

Enlarged View

One of the smallest and darkest moons in our solar system, potato-shaped Phobos was probably an asteroid captured by the planet it orbits. Its gravity is so weak that if you visited Phobos, you'd only weigh as much as a mouse!

▶

Ganymede

This moon is the biggest one in our solar system, even larger than the planet Mercury. Unlike our Moon, Ganymede doesn't have deep craters or tall mountains—these get wiped out by the constant shifting of Ganymede's icy crust.

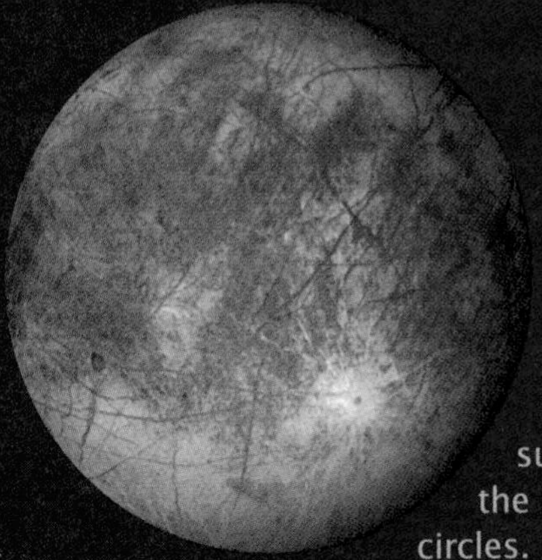

◀ Europa

This ice-covered moon might have oceans of water beneath its surface, heated by energy from the pull of the enormous planet it circles. NASA is currently developing a robot probe that will drill below the ice and send a submarine with a remote-control camera to explore the depths!

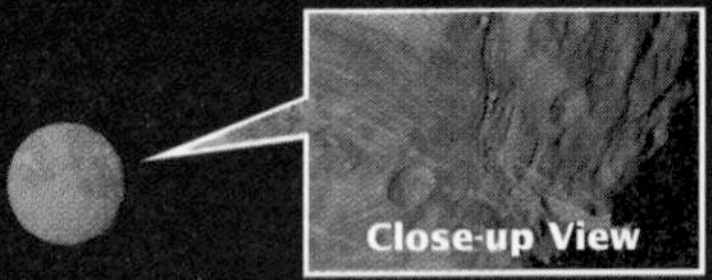

Close-up View

▶

Miranda

This moon circles a very boring-looking planet, but *it* sure doesn't look boring! Miranda is covered in a strange mix of grooves, cliffs, and valleys. Scientists think this moon might have split apart and reformed several times during its history!

Io ▶

Io has the most active volcanoes of any moon or planet in our solar system. Even though it's over half a billion miles from the Sun, it's the hottest moon in the solar system!

COMETS!

Ever throw a dirty snowball? A big one? Well, this final stop on your solar system tour will take you to the home of the biggest dirty snowballs you've ever seen: **comets**!

These lumps of ice, dust, and rock get a *lot* more mileage than the average snowball, though—unless you can throw a snowball that does laps around the Sun!

COMET CLUSTERS

Comets come from one of two regions: the Kuiper Belt or the Oort Cloud. The Kuiper Belt can be found just past Neptune (remember this region from page 38?), and the Oort Cloud is even farther out—it contains the most distant objects that orbit our Sun.

Every so often, one of the ice chunks gets tugged away from the crowd and starts whizzing toward the Sun. As the comet gets closer to the Sun, it grows *two* long tails!

WHY TWO TAILS?

The comet grows its tails because it *melts* as it gets closer to the Sun. Dust from the comet spews off and trails behind it in a glowing stream that stretches up to 90 million miles (145 million km)! Meanwhile, the frozen gas in the comet evaporates and forms the second tail, which gets blown away from the comet by radiation from the Sun (so this tail always points away from the Sun). Eventually, the comet will lose all of its gas and dust and break apart completely.

If the comet's orbit takes it close enough to Earth, its glowing tails can be seen streaking across the night sky. It's an impressive sight— check it out for yourself with your Cosmic Viewer!

COSMIC VIEWER

DISC 2, IMAGE 7

Catch a glimpse of a comet and its two tails!

This is the comet Hale-Bopp, which passed near Earth in 1997. Can you see how the two tails of the comet go in different directions in your 3-D view?

Gas tail

Dust tail

Well, cadet, now that you've toured our solar system, where to next? Are there other planets in other solar systems, just waiting to be discovered?

Sure thing! Planets that orbit other stars are called *exoplanets*, and scientists (like the one you'll meet on the next page) have already discovered lots of them. How? By looking for wobbly stars!

WHAT MAKES A STAR WOBBLE?

A star's gravity keeps a planet in orbit, but the planet also tugs back on the star—and this tug-o-war makes the star wobble a little. Planet hunters can predict the size of the exoplanet by studying the star's movement. It's just tough to actually *see* the exoplanet because of all the bright starlight around it.

Astronomers have found over a hundred exoplanets (just in the last decade!), and they're planning a series of missions that will help them discover even more. In 2009, a new space telescope called *SIM* will study distant stars and search for Earth-like planets out there!

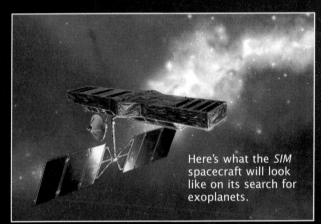

Here's what the *SIM* spacecraft will look like on its search for exoplanets.

QuickBlast

Stumbling Star

Want to see why stars wobble when planets orbit them? Then try this!

1 Ask an Intergalactic Adult (IGA) to stand facing you. The IGA is a star, and you're a planet.

2 Now start orbiting your star: Hold hands and spin around the IGA. Do you notice that the IGA sometimes has to take a step away from his or her spot for balance? That's the idea— your orbit makes your star wobble!

Dr. Ben Oppenheimer
PLANET HUNTER

Here's the inside story on exoplanets from planet hunter Ben R. Oppenheimer, an astrophysics research fellow at the American Museum of Natural History in New York City.

Question: How many exoplanets are out there?

Answer: We've found more than a hundred so far. This is a huge change for astronomy. Only ten years ago, not a single exoplanet was known to exist. The problem, though, is that we haven't actually seen any exoplanets. We've used the wobbling of the stars they orbit to find out about them.

Q: Why can't we actually see any exoplanets?

A: The stars that they orbit (their suns) are hundreds of millions of times brighter than the exoplanets, so the exoplanets get lost in the glare from the star.

Q: What can be done about the starlight?

A: Well, a number of things, but I am trying to block it. If you watch a plane flying through the sky and it gets close to the Sun, you can't see the plane unless you hold up your hand to block out the sunlight. We're doing the same thing with these stars.

Q: How do you do that?

A: We've made an instrument, like a camera, that attaches to a big telescope in Hawaii. The camera has a small piece of metal in it that is just the right size to block out a star, but let you see faint things next to the star.

Q: Which stars are you studying?

A: About 300 of the brightest and nearest stars. We have to use bright stars because of the way the camera works, and we want the closest stars because the planets will be easier to see.

Q: How did you get interested in hunting for exoplanets?

A: To tell the truth: *Star Trek.* I loved it when I was a kid, and I've always found space exploration fascinating. I really want to see what exoplanets are like. Also, maybe in the future we will be able to tell whether there is life on those planets. Who knows what we'll find? I hope we find really strange planets that no one has ever imagined before.

DESIGN YOUR OWN PLANET!

It's amazing to think that there are untold numbers of planets orbiting other stars in the universe. What do you think they might look like? Here's your chance to use your knowledge of the planets in *our* solar system to create your own brand-new worlds!

Launch Objective

> Design a planet that might exist somewhere in the universe!

Your equipment

▶ Colored pencils or crayons

Mission Procedure

Part 1: Terrestrial Planet

Remember: A terrestrial planet is a planet that has a surface that can be landed on, like Earth and Mars, for example.

1 Start your terrestrial planet by drawing a circle on your paper.

2 Now decide on your planet's atmosphere.

■ No atmosphere?

If your planet is really small, it won't have enough gravity to hold on to gases. That means it'll have lots of craters on its surface, like Mercury.

With no atmosphere, your planet will get pummeled by space rocks, and the craters will stick around for a long time because there's no weather to erode them.

■ Thick atmosphere?

Does your planet have a thick atmosphere like Venus's? If so, draw lots of clouds—you won't be able to see your planet's surface.

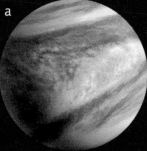

■ Thinner atmosphere?

If your planet has a thinner atmosphere (like Earth and Mars do), you'll be able to see the surface. What will it look like?

Rust on the surface of your planet would look reddish orange, like Mars.

Are there clouds floating above your planet's surface?

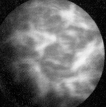

Lava pouring out of volcanoes could create glowing spots!

Frozen water—or almost any sort of frozen gas—will create pale spots on your planet. Your planet could have frozen ice caps on its poles.

3 If there's liquid water on your planet, there might also be life! What signs of life can you imagine?

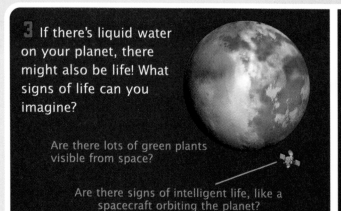

Are there lots of green plants visible from space?

Are there signs of intelligent life, like a spacecraft orbiting the planet?

4 Now for the finishing touches: Give your planet a moon...or two...or more!

Part 2: Gas Giant

1 Just like before, start by drawing a circle. But remember—your gas giant should be a lot bigger than your terrestrial planet!

If there's methane in the atmosphere, your planet could look bright blue like Neptune.

2 What color is the atmosphere of your gas giant? The color (or colors) will depend on the gases your planet contains. You can see some possible colors below.

Phosphorus and sulfur could create yellowish orange or even pinkish red!

3 Does your planet have different-colored stripes? Make sure they go in the same direction that your planet rotates.

4 If your planet's winds create giant storms, draw a swirling spot like the Great Red Spot on Jupiter.

5 The gas giants in our solar system all have rings. Does your planet have big, bright rings like Saturn, or thin, faint rings like Jupiter, Uranus, and Neptune? Like the stripes, the rings should go in the same direction your planet rotates.

6 Just one last touch: Outside of your planet's rings, add lots of moons. Remember that Jupiter has more than sixty moons!

More from Mission Control

To design more planets, head over to the Space U web site at www.scholastic.com/space. There you can pick all the features of your planet, see its moons in orbit, and post your creation to the Space U bulletin board!

A planet's stripes always go in the same direction as its rotation.

Sulfur combined with other ingredients might even make a planet look greenish.

Your planet could have wide, bright rings.

NEXT STOP: Your Choice!

Congrats, cadet! You've completed your grand tour of our solar system, and you have plenty of fuel to imagine what lies beyond!

What will you explore next? There's *lots* left to discover about planets, moons, comets, asteroids, and more—think of the headlines that could be on the horizon!

UNIVERSE TODAY
PROBE LANDS ON PLUTO!

SPACE SENTINEL
SCIENTISTS GLIMPSE EARTH-LIKE PLANET ORBITING DISTANT STAR!

COSMIC TIMES
ASTRONAUTS SET FOOT ON MARS!

PLANETARY POST
ROBOT DRILLS BENEATH EUROPA'S ICE!

Of course, these are just a *few* of the possibilities! What else can you imagine? And what kinds of great discoveries could have *your* name on them?

That's for you to think about as you wait for your next package from Space U. So, until next month, keep your thrusters burning and stay cosmically cool!

THE ANSWER STATION

- **Page 12: Size Up the Solar System!**
  3) Mercury, Venus, and Pluto are poppy seeds. Earth and Mars are peppercorns. Neptune and Uranus are coffee beans. Saturn is the almond, and Jupiter is the walnut.

- **Pages 26–27: Mars Match Up**
  1) E 2) I 3) H 4) B 5) D 6) F 7) A
  8) G 9) J 10) C

- **Page 29: Spot the Dot**

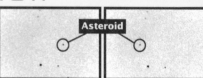

Asteroid

- **Pages 40–41: Moon Match**
  1) **Mars**: Phobos. 2) **Jupiter**: Io, Ganymede, and Europa. 3) **Saturn**: Titan. 4) **Uranus**: Miranda.
  5) **Neptune**: Triton.